PRINCEWILL LAGANG

The Marriage Mindset: Fostering Growth Together

First published by PRINCEWILL LAGANG 2023

Copyright © 2023 by Princewill Lagang

All rights reserved. No part of this publication may be reproduced, stored or transmitted in any form or by any means, electronic, mechanical, photocopying, recording, scanning, or otherwise without written permission from the publisher. It is illegal to copy this book, post it to a website, or distribute it by any other means without permission.

Princewill Lagang asserts the moral right to be identified as the author of this work.

First edition

This book was professionally typeset on Reedsy.
Find out more at reedsy.com

Contents

1. The Marriage Mindset and the Path to Lasting Partnerships — 1
2. Embracing Change and Adaptability for Lasting Love — 3
3. The Lifeline of Love: Continuous Communication and... — 6
4. Nurturing Growth Together: Cultivating Mutual Support in... — 9
5. Strengthened Through Storms: Navigating Challenges and... — 12
6. Flourishing Together: Fostering Individual Growth within a... — 15
7. Weaving Tomorrow Together: Building Shared Dreams and Goals — 18
8. The Heartfelt Connection: Emotional Intelligence and Empathy — 21
9. Embracing the Unknown: Taking Risks and Exploring New... — 24
10. Embracing the Heartbeat of Love: Nurturing Intimacy and... — 27
11. Lessons in Resilience: Learning from Mistakes and Failures — 30
12. The Ever-Unfolding Tale: Embracing the Journey of Growth... — 33

1

The Marriage Mindset and the Path to Lasting Partnerships

In the journey of love and companionship, there exists a fundamental concept that forms the bedrock of every successful relationship: the marriage mindset. This mindset transcends the mere act of getting married; it delves deep into the attitudes, beliefs, and behaviors that shape our connections with our partners.

At its core, the marriage mindset encompasses a holistic approach to nurturing a relationship, emphasizing growth, adaptability, and continuous evolution. It's about understanding that the path to a lasting partnership is not linear but is instead marked by twists, turns, and opportunities for both personal and collective development.

In a world where change is constant and challenges are inevitable, the marriage mindset serves as a compass that guides couples through the turbulent waters of life. It encourages partners to view challenges as opportunities for growth, rather than as obstacles to be avoided. This mindset embraces the idea that a strong relationship isn't built on the absence of problems, but on the ability to navigate them together.

Throughout this journey, the concept of growth and evolution takes center stage. Relationships, like individuals, have the capacity to learn, adapt, and transform. Just as we, as individuals, aspire to become better versions of ourselves, so too should our partnerships strive for growth and development.

By adopting the marriage mindset, couples cultivate a shared sense of purpose, one that centers on mutual support, emotional connection, and shared goals. This mindset encourages partners to communicate openly, empathize deeply, and be willing to learn from each other's perspectives.

In the chapters that follow, we will explore the various facets of the marriage mindset and delve into practical strategies for integrating this approach into your own relationship. We will unravel the power of embracing change, nurturing personal development, and embracing the ebb and flow of life as a team.

As you embark on this journey of discovery and introspection, remember that the marriage mindset is not a destination but a lifelong commitment to fostering a partnership that stands the test of time. So, let us dive into the heart of the matter, exploring how the marriage mindset can transform relationships and pave the way for enduring love and companionship.

2

Embracing Change and Adaptability for Lasting Love

In the realm of relationships, change is not an adversary to be resisted; rather, it is a constant companion that presents opportunities for growth, understanding, and deeper connection. In this chapter, we will unravel the significance of embracing change and adapting as a couple, and how cultivating a growth-oriented mindset enhances the resilience of your partnership.

The Dance of Change:
Change is an inevitable force that shapes our lives, challenging us to evolve and learn. When it comes to relationships, change can manifest in various forms—career transitions, shifting priorities, family dynamics, and personal growth journeys. Rather than fearing change, couples who thrive understand that it is the rhythm of life itself. Embracing change as a joint adventure enables partners to develop a shared sense of adaptability and a renewed perspective on each other.

The Power of Adaptability:

Adaptability is the secret sauce that keeps relationships strong and vibrant. Couples who can flex and adjust in response to changing circumstances find themselves better equipped to weather the storms that life inevitably brings. Embracing adaptability doesn't mean compromising one's identity or values; rather, it involves being open to redefining roles, expectations, and even relationship dynamics as necessary. This willingness to adapt fosters an environment of mutual understanding and support.

A Growth-Oriented Mindset:

Central to embracing change and adaptability is the cultivation of a growth-oriented mindset. A growth mindset encourages partners to view challenges as stepping stones rather than stumbling blocks. This perspective recognizes that setbacks and uncertainties are opportunities for learning, improvement, and strengthening the partnership's foundation. Partners who approach difficulties with curiosity and a desire to learn not only foster their own personal development but also enhance the resilience of the relationship.

Enhancing Resilience Through Growth:

A growth-oriented mindset bolsters the resilience of a relationship by instilling a sense of purpose and unity in the face of adversity. Couples who view challenges as chances to grow together are better equipped to navigate difficult times with grace and patience. This resilience is not born out of avoiding difficulties but from confronting them head-on, armed with the belief that every challenge is an opportunity for mutual development and understanding.

In the chapters that follow, we will delve into practical strategies for integrating adaptability into your relationship. We will explore effective communication techniques, ways to approach change with an open heart, and methods to encourage each other's personal growth.

Remember, change is not a disruption of your love story; it is a narrative arc that adds depth, richness, and character to the journey. By embracing change and nurturing adaptability, you can craft a partnership that thrives amidst life's ever-evolving landscape. So, let us embark on this exploration of adaptability, where we discover the art of dancing with change and nurturing a love that evolves gracefully.

3

The Lifeline of Love: Continuous Communication and Connection

I n the tapestry of a marriage, communication stands as the threads that weave together emotions, thoughts, and shared experiences. This chapter delves into the pivotal role of ongoing communication in nurturing a healthy and thriving partnership. We'll explore the art of maintaining emotional closeness and understanding through effective strategies.

Communication: The Heartbeat of Connection:
Communication is the lifeblood of any relationship. It is the means through which partners express their feelings, share their joys and concerns, and create a shared language unique to their bond. Effective communication is not just about talking; it's about active listening, empathy, and understanding. In a world filled with distractions, taking the time to engage in deep, meaningful conversations becomes a cornerstone of lasting love.

The Dance of Emotional Intimacy:
Emotional closeness is nurtured through genuine communication that goes

beyond surface-level exchanges. It involves sharing vulnerabilities, dreams, and fears. When partners feel safe to open up about their innermost thoughts, a profound emotional connection blossoms. This emotional intimacy is built upon a foundation of trust, where each partner feels valued and heard.

Strategies for Sustaining Connection:

1. Regular Check-Ins: Set aside dedicated time for conversations where you catch up on each other's lives, thoughts, and feelings. These check-ins provide a safe space for sharing and staying attuned to each other's emotional states.

2. Active Listening: Practice active listening by giving your full attention to your partner when they speak. Validate their emotions and avoid interrupting. This fosters an atmosphere of mutual respect and understanding.

3. Empathy and Validation: Empathize with your partner's experiences and emotions. Validate their feelings even if you don't share the same perspective. This creates a supportive environment where both partners feel valued.

4. Open and Honest Expression: Encourage an environment where both partners feel comfortable expressing their thoughts without fear of judgment. Honesty lays the foundation for trust and transparency.

5. Nonverbal Communication: Remember that communication extends beyond words. Body language, gestures, and facial expressions can convey volumes. Pay attention to these cues to better understand your partner's emotions.

6. Conflict Resolution: Learn to navigate disagreements with respect and empathy. Effective communication during times of conflict helps prevent misunderstandings from escalating.

7. Shared Activities: Engage in activities that encourage shared experiences.

These shared moments create opportunities for natural conversations to unfold.

The Beauty of Unwavering Connection:
As partners commit to continuous communication, they embark on a journey that deepens their connection over time. Through shared conversations, moments of vulnerability, and mutual understanding, they create a space where their love can flourish.

In the chapters ahead, we will explore how communication extends into every aspect of a relationship, from resolving conflicts to celebrating triumphs. By mastering the art of ongoing communication and sustaining emotional closeness, you will fortify your partnership with a bond that only strengthens with time. So, let us delve into the intricacies of communication, where the threads of connection are intricately woven, creating a tapestry of enduring love.

4

Nurturing Growth Together: Cultivating Mutual Support in Your Relationship

In the garden of love, mutual support is the nourishing sunlight that allows each partner's individuality and aspirations to flourish. This chapter delves into the profound significance of supporting each other's personal growth and goals within the context of a relationship. We'll explore how to create an environment that fosters encouragement, empowerment, and shared dreams.

Championing Individuality:
A thriving relationship is one in which partners not only recognize but also celebrate each other's unique qualities, passions, and ambitions. Encouraging individual growth doesn't fragment the partnership; rather, it enriches it. Partners who feel supported in pursuing their personal goals often bring a renewed sense of energy and enthusiasm back to the relationship.

The Power of Encouragement:
Support goes beyond mere acknowledgment—it's about actively uplifting and motivating each other. Encouragement involves celebrating successes,

no matter how small, and providing a safe space to discuss setbacks and challenges. When partners act as each other's cheerleaders, the relationship transforms into a hub of positivity and inspiration.

Creating an Empowering Environment:
1. Open Dialogue: Initiate conversations about each other's dreams and aspirations. Understand the motivations behind these goals and offer your unwavering belief in their potential to achieve them.

2. Shared Vision: Identify areas where your individual goals align and complement each other. This shared vision creates a foundation for mutual encouragement and collaboration.

3. Active Participation: Participate in each other's pursuits when possible. Attend events, offer assistance, or simply lend a listening ear. Your involvement signifies genuine interest and investment in each other's growth.

4. Problem Solving: When challenges arise, approach them as a team. Brainstorm solutions, offer insights, and provide emotional support during difficult times.

5. Celebrating Milestones: Recognize and celebrate achievements, no matter how small. Your enthusiasm reinforces the idea that both partners' successes are equally valuable and worth celebrating.

6. Constructive Feedback: When seeking feedback, provide it in a constructive and supportive manner. Your insights should inspire growth, not deter it.

Shared Dreams, Stronger Bonds:
When both partners actively nurture each other's growth, the relationship becomes a catalyst for personal development. Supporting each other's endeavors creates a sense of unity, where challenges are faced together and

victories are celebrated as a team.

In the chapters that follow, we'll explore the harmony between personal aspirations and collective dreams. We'll delve into the art of collaboration, where the sparks of individual creativity combine to create a shared flame of purpose. By cultivating an environment of mutual support, you'll weave a narrative of love that thrives on each other's growth and empowerment. So, let us journey into the heart of partnership, where the soil of support nurtures aspirations and love blossoms in the light of encouragement.

5

Strengthened Through Storms: Navigating Challenges and Conflict in a Growth-Oriented Relationship

In the tapestry of a growth-oriented relationship, challenges and conflicts are the threads that add depth, resilience, and character. This chapter delves into the pivotal role of challenges and conflict in fostering growth and understanding within a partnership. We'll explore strategies for navigating disagreements constructively, transforming conflicts into opportunities for mutual learning and connection.

The Crucible of Growth:
   Challenges and conflicts are not adversaries to be avoided; they are catalysts for growth. In a growth-oriented relationship, partners recognize that adversity provides a chance to learn, adapt, and strengthen their bond. Embracing challenges as avenues for personal and collective development allows couples to evolve together, rather than being hindered by obstacles.

Conflict as a Pathway to Understanding:

Conflict is a natural expression of differing viewpoints, needs, and desires. In a growth-oriented partnership, conflicts are reframed as opportunities for deeper understanding. When partners approach disagreements with empathy and a desire to find common ground, conflicts transform from divisive battles into bridges of connection.

Strategies for Constructive Conflict Resolution:

1. Stay Calm: In the heat of an argument, emotions can run high. Practice emotional self-regulation to ensure that conflicts are approached with a clear and level-headed mindset.

2. Active Listening: Truly listen to your partner's perspective without interrupting. Seek to understand their feelings and concerns before expressing your own viewpoint.

3. Empathy and Validation: Show empathy by acknowledging your partner's emotions, even if you don't share the same perspective. Validating their feelings creates an atmosphere of mutual respect.

4. Use "I" Statements: Express your feelings and concerns using "I" statements to avoid sounding accusatory. This encourages open communication and prevents defensiveness.

5. Focus on Solutions: Instead of dwelling on the problem, shift the focus to finding solutions. Collaborate to identify compromises that work for both partners.

6. Take Breaks: If a conflict escalates, take a break to cool off and regain perspective. This prevents discussions from spiraling into harmful exchanges.

7. Seek Common Ground: Identify areas of agreement and shared values. Working from common ground lays the foundation for constructive problem-solving.

8. Learn from Conflict: After resolving a conflict, reflect on what you've learned about each other and the dynamics of your relationship. Use this knowledge to grow and prevent similar conflicts in the future.

The Beauty of Resolution:

Growth-oriented relationships are not devoid of conflicts; they're marked by the ability to navigate disagreements with respect, empathy, and a commitment to mutual understanding. As partners learn to embrace challenges as opportunities for growth, they create a relationship that deepens in wisdom, compassion, and shared resilience.

In the chapters ahead, we'll explore the intricate dance of conflict and resolution, where disagreements become stepping stones to a stronger bond. By mastering the art of constructive conflict resolution, you will forge a path that transforms challenges into triumphs and disagreements into deeper connection. So, let us venture into the heart of conflict, where growth takes root, and love emerges even stronger from the storms of life.

6

Flourishing Together: Fostering Individual Growth within a Shared Partnership

In the intricate tapestry of a flourishing marriage, individual growth is the vibrant thread that weaves together the fabric of shared dreams. This chapter delves into the delicate balance between personal growth and shared partnership goals. We'll explore how pursuing individual interests not only contributes to a thriving marriage but also enriches the journey of love.

Harmony of Self and Partnership:
A thriving relationship acknowledges the importance of maintaining one's individuality while nurturing the collective bond. Partners who recognize and encourage each other's personal growth create a harmonious dance between the self and the partnership. This balance fosters an environment where both individuals can pursue their passions and aspirations, elevating the relationship to new heights.

The Gift of Personal Fulfillment:

Pursuing individual interests brings a sense of fulfillment that radiates into the relationship. When partners are engaged in activities that bring them joy and purpose, they become more content and self-aware. This personal fulfillment translates into a positive energy that infuses the partnership, enhancing the overall quality of the relationship.

Strategies for Fostering Individual Growth:

1. Open Dialogue: Initiate conversations about each other's personal goals and interests. Share your dreams and aspirations with enthusiasm, inviting your partner to do the same.

2. Supportive Space: Create an environment where pursuing individual interests is encouraged and celebrated. Provide time and space for each other to engage in activities that bring personal satisfaction.

3. Shared Values: Identify shared values and passions that can be integrated into your individual pursuits. This allows for a connection between personal growth and shared partnership goals.

4. Balance and Boundaries: Strive for a balance between personal endeavors and shared commitments. Establish healthy boundaries to ensure that personal growth does not overshadow the partnership.

5. Collaborative Growth: Explore opportunities for collaborative growth, where both partners can engage in joint pursuits that align with their individual interests.

6. Celebrate Milestones: Acknowledge and celebrate each other's achievements and milestones in personal growth. Your genuine excitement reinforces the importance of individual development.

Elevating Love through Individual Flourishment:

When partners actively support each other's individual growth, the relationship becomes a haven where each person is encouraged to reach their fullest potential. By nurturing personal passions and aspirations, couples infuse their partnership with a sense of dynamism, enthusiasm, and a shared commitment to evolving together.

In the chapters that follow, we'll explore the symphony between individuality and partnership, where each partner's growth contributes to the harmony of the relationship. By embracing personal development within the context of shared dreams, you'll create a love story that radiates with the brilliance of individual authenticity and shared connection. So, let us venture into the realm of personal fulfillment, where individual growth becomes the melody that enriches the chorus of love.

7

Weaving Tomorrow Together: Building Shared Dreams and Goals

In the canvas of a lasting relationship, shared dreams and goals are the vibrant strokes that paint a picture of a future intertwined with love and purpose. This chapter delves into the process of crafting and pursuing shared dreams and aspirations. We'll explore the art of aligning goals and priorities as a couple, creating a roadmap that leads to a fulfilling and harmonious life journey.

The Beauty of Shared Dreams:
Shared dreams breathe life into a relationship, providing a common purpose that fuels the partnership's growth. Partners who create a vision for their future cultivate a sense of unity and direction that propels them forward, even in the face of challenges. These shared dreams are a testament to the power of love that transcends individual ambitions and embraces the collective power of "us."

The Art of Alignment:
Aligning goals and priorities requires open communication, mutual un-

derstanding, and a willingness to compromise. Partners who successfully integrate their individual dreams into a shared vision create a foundation of shared purpose, where both individuals work together to achieve their joint aspirations.

Techniques for Aligning Goals:
1. Shared Values: Identify core values that both partners hold dear. These values become guiding principles that shape your shared dreams and goals.

2. Visioning Exercises: Set aside time to envision your ideal future as a couple. Discuss your hopes, aspirations, and what you wish to accomplish together.

3. Compromise and Collaboration: Be open to compromise when needed and collaborate on finding common ground. Balancing individual aspirations with shared goals requires give-and-take.

4. Break Down Goals: Divide larger goals into smaller, manageable steps. This makes the journey towards your shared dreams feel achievable and less daunting.

5. Regular Check-Ins: Periodically revisit your shared dreams and goals to ensure that you're on track. This also provides an opportunity to adjust your plans as circumstances change.

6. Celebrate Milestones: Celebrate achievements along the way, both big and small. Acknowledging progress fosters motivation and a sense of accomplishment.

The Tapestry of Togetherness:
Building shared dreams and goals is a journey that transforms the relationship into a collaborative masterpiece. As partners commit to walking this path hand in hand, they create a legacy of shared experiences, mutual achievements, and a sense of accomplishment that only grows with time.

In the chapters ahead, we'll explore the enchanting blend of individual aspirations and shared dreams, where the power of unity paves the way to a fulfilling future. By crafting a vision that harmonizes personal ambitions with collective purpose, you'll create a love story that stands as a testament to the beauty of shared dreams and goals. So, let us step into the realm of possibility, where shared visions guide us towards a horizon illuminated by the brilliance of love.

8

The Heartfelt Connection: Emotional Intelligence and Empathy

In the intricate mosaic of a thriving relationship, emotional intelligence and empathy are the delicate brushstrokes that create a masterpiece of understanding and connection. This chapter delves into the profound significance of emotional intelligence in comprehending each other's inner worlds. We'll also explore how empathy serves as the bridge that fosters connection, vulnerability, and mutual growth.

Embracing Emotional Intelligence:
Emotional intelligence is the ability to recognize, understand, and manage emotions—both one's own and those of others. In a relationship, partners who cultivate emotional intelligence create an environment where feelings are acknowledged and respected. This awareness is the cornerstone of effective communication, conflict resolution, and overall relationship satisfaction.

The Power of Empathy:
Empathy is the art of stepping into another person's shoes and truly understanding their feelings and perspectives. In a growth-oriented relationship,

empathy fosters a profound connection where partners feel seen, heard, and validated. Empathy serves as a beacon of support during challenging times, nurturing a bond that thrives on mutual understanding.

Techniques for Cultivating Emotional Intelligence and Empathy:
   1. Self-Awareness: Reflect on your own emotions, triggers, and reactions. Self-awareness is the foundation upon which emotional intelligence is built.

2. Active Listening: Pay full attention when your partner speaks, observing both their words and nonverbal cues. Active listening demonstrates that their feelings matter to you.

3. Validation: Validate your partner's emotions by acknowledging their feelings, even if you don't share the same perspective. This validates their experiences and fosters trust.

4. Mirror and Validate: Reflect back what you hear to ensure that you've understood your partner correctly. This practice minimizes misinterpretations and misunderstandings.

5. Empathetic Response: Respond to your partner's emotions with empathy, showing that you understand and care about their feelings. Offer support and encouragement.

6. Non-Judgmental Attitude: Approach your partner's emotions without judgment. Creating a safe space for emotional expression encourages openness and vulnerability.

The Tapestry of Understanding:
   Emotional intelligence and empathy weave a tapestry of understanding that enriches the fabric of a relationship. Partners who prioritize these qualities create an atmosphere where feelings are cherished, misunderstandings are minimized, and bonds are strengthened through mutual empathy.

THE HEARTFELT CONNECTION: EMOTIONAL INTELLIGENCE AND EMPATHY

In the chapters to come, we'll delve into the depths of emotional intimacy and empathy, where partners learn to connect on a heart level. By nurturing emotional intelligence and practicing empathy, you'll forge a love story that thrives on deep connection, authentic communication, and mutual growth. So, let us explore the realm of emotional understanding, where empathy forms the bridge to a love that resonates with compassion and understanding.

9

Embracing the Unknown: Taking Risks and Exploring New Horizons Together

In the tapestry of a vibrant partnership, the threads of growth are woven by the hands of couples who dare to step beyond the familiar and into the realm of the unknown. This chapter delves into the profound significance of taking risks and embracing new experiences as a couple. We'll explore how venturing outside comfort zones not only invigorates the relationship but also forges bonds that are marked by shared courage and adventure.

The Call of the Uncharted:

Stepping outside comfort zones is a testament to a couple's shared determination to explore, evolve, and grow. It is an acknowledgment that the journey of love is not confined to the safety of routines, but is an exhilarating quest that invites partners to rise above limitations and embrace the excitement of the unknown.

The Connection Through Novelty:

Trying new experiences together is akin to penning fresh chapters in the story of your relationship. It ignites passion, curiosity, and shared memories that deepen the connection. When couples venture into uncharted territories, they create a tapestry of shared adventures, reminding them of their ability to overcome challenges together.

Techniques for Embracing New Experiences:
1. Shared Bucket List: Create a list of experiences you both wish to try, whether it's travel, hobbies, or personal goals. Work together to make these dreams a reality.

2. Encourage Exploration: Motivate each other to step outside your comfort zones by providing unwavering support and encouragement.

3. Face Fears Together: Confront fears and challenges as a team. Whether it's public speaking, outdoor activities, or learning a new skill, facing fears together fosters unity and resilience.

4. Celebrate Small Wins: Acknowledge and celebrate each other's efforts and achievements, even if they seem minor. This reinforces the idea that taking risks is a journey worth celebrating.

5. Reflect on Experiences: After trying new things, reflect on the experiences you've shared. Discuss the lessons learned and the memories created. This strengthens the connection and encourages further exploration.

The Canvas of Adventure:
Venturing beyond comfort zones is not only about the activities themselves; it's about the story that unfolds when partners choose to explore together. These shared experiences serve as touchstones, reminding couples of their capacity for courage, growth, and unity in the face of the unknown.

In the upcoming chapters, we'll dive into the realm of shared adventures and the journey of discovery that strengthens the bond between partners.

By embracing the thrill of the new and the unexplored, you'll weave a love story that is rich in spontaneity, shared memories, and the joy of embarking on life's daring escapades side by side. So, let us embark on the journey of exploration, where stepping outside comfort zones becomes the brush that paints a portrait of shared courage and vibrant connection.

10

Embracing the Heartbeat of Love: Nurturing Intimacy and Affection

In the symphony of a growth-oriented marriage, intimacy and affection are the harmonious notes that resonate with passion, connection, and vulnerability. This chapter delves into the profound significance of nurturing intimacy and physical affection as cornerstones of a thriving relationship. We'll explore the art of fostering a strong romantic bond that deepens with time, allowing love to blossom in its most authentic and tender form.

The Essence of Intimacy:
Intimacy goes beyond physical closeness; it is the emotional, intellectual, and spiritual connection that two people share. In a growth-oriented marriage, partners recognize the importance of cultivating intimacy in all its dimensions. Intimate moments serve as the glue that binds hearts together, fostering a sense of safety, trust, and belonging.

The Language of Physical Affection:
Physical affection is a language spoken through touch—a tender embrace,

a gentle caress, or a shared moment of warmth. These gestures express love, desire, and the unspoken emotions that words often struggle to convey. In a growth-oriented relationship, physical affection is a bridge that connects partners, reinforcing their bond and nurturing emotional closeness.

Techniques for Nurturing Intimacy and Affection:
1. Quality Time: Spend dedicated time together, free from distractions, to nurture deep conversations, shared experiences, and intimate connections.

2. Physical Touch: Express affection through physical touch, whether it's holding hands, hugging, cuddling, or playful gestures that communicate love and tenderness.

3. Open Communication: Engage in open discussions about your desires, preferences, and boundaries when it comes to physical intimacy. This ensures that both partners feel comfortable and understood.

4. Surprise Gestures: Surprise each other with thoughtful gestures that show you're thinking of them. Small acts of kindness and consideration go a long way in nurturing affection.

5. Spontaneous Moments: Embrace spontaneous displays of affection. These unexpected moments of closeness infuse the relationship with an air of excitement and passion.

6. Shared Rituals: Develop shared rituals that hold significance for your relationship. These rituals create a sense of intimacy and connection, serving as anchors in the daily routine.

The Melody of Connection:
Nurturing intimacy and affection is a journey that adds depth, passion, and authenticity to a marriage. Partners who prioritize these elements create a relationship that is marked by tenderness, closeness, and a continuous spark

that burns brightly over time.

In the upcoming chapters, we'll delve into the realm of enduring love and the intricacies of maintaining a thriving romantic bond. By embracing the language of intimacy and the art of physical affection, you'll craft a love story that resonates with a harmony of hearts, an embrace of vulnerability, and a celebration of the profound connection that only grows stronger with every touch. So, let us immerse ourselves in the world of tenderness, where intimacy becomes the melody that serenades the dance of love.

11

Lessons in Resilience: Learning from Mistakes and Failures

In the intricate mosaic of a growth-oriented relationship, mistakes and failures are not blemishes to be hidden; they are stepping stones to personal and relational evolution. This chapter delves into the profound significance of learning from missteps and failures, both as individuals and as a couple. We'll explore how embracing challenges with a positive mindset fosters resilience, wisdom, and an unwavering commitment to mutual growth.

The Canvas of Growth:
Mistakes and failures are not roadblocks; they are signposts pointing towards opportunities for growth. In a growth-oriented relationship, partners understand that setbacks are not failures but are instead lessons waiting to be learned. These experiences contribute to the rich tapestry of their journey, adding depth, understanding, and strength.

Nurturing Resilience:
Resilience is the ability to bounce back from challenges, stronger and wiser.

LESSONS IN RESILIENCE: LEARNING FROM MISTAKES AND FAILURES

When couples embrace mistakes and failures as part of their journey, they foster an environment of shared resilience. Partners who weather storms together develop a deep bond founded on the belief that they can face anything life throws at them.

Techniques for Learning and Growing from Mistakes:

1. Reframe "Failures": Shift your perspective on failures. Instead of viewing them as defeats, consider them as stepping stones toward growth and learning.

2. Reflect and Learn: After a setback, take time to reflect on what went wrong and what could be done differently. These reflections offer valuable insights for personal and relational improvement.

3. Supportive Communication: Encourage open discussions about failures without blame or judgment. Create a safe space where both partners can share their experiences and learn from each other.

4. Positive Mindset: Approach challenges with a positive mindset. Cultivate the belief that every obstacle is an opportunity for growth and a chance to enhance the relationship.

5. Set Realistic Expectations: Understand that perfection is not attainable. Mistakes are a natural part of the journey, and acknowledging this prevents unnecessary pressure and disappointment.

6. Celebrate Progress: Acknowledge and celebrate the progress made, even if it's incremental. These victories, no matter how small, are significant steps toward growth.

The Tapestry of Wisdom:

Learning from mistakes and failures enriches the relationship with depth and insight. Partners who navigate challenges with resilience and a positive outlook create a tapestry woven with the threads of wisdom, understanding, and shared determination.

In the upcoming chapters, we'll delve into the realm of lasting love and the art of weathering life's storms as a united front. By embracing challenges with a growth-oriented perspective, you'll forge a love story that stands as a testament to the power of resilience, learning, and the boundless potential that blooms from the soil of shared experiences. So, let us embark on the journey of growth, where mistakes become stepping stones and failures become the fertile ground from which love grows stronger.

12

The Ever-Unfolding Tale: Embracing the Journey of Growth Together

As we come to the culmination of this exploration, we find ourselves immersed in the beauty of a growth-oriented marriage—a partnership that thrives on evolution, connection, and shared dreams. This final chapter reflects on the transformation that a marriage mindset rooted in growth brings to the tapestry of love. We'll summarize key takeaways and offer guidance to readers as they embark on their own journey of cultivating the marriage mindset.

The Blossoming of Love:

A growth-oriented marriage is a testament to the power of adaptability, empathy, and mutual evolution. It's a commitment to embracing change as a catalyst for deeper connection, facing challenges as opportunities for growth, and cherishing shared experiences that enrich the relationship. This mindset allows love to not just survive, but to flourish amidst the ever-changing landscape of life.

Key Takeaways from Our Journey:

1. Embrace Change: Change is a constant in life. Instead of fearing it, embrace it as a shared adventure that strengthens your bond.

2. Cultivate Empathy: Empathy is the bridge that connects hearts. Cultivate the ability to understand each other's feelings and perspectives.

3. Foster Communication: Ongoing communication is the lifeblood of a relationship. Create a space for deep conversations and open discussions.

4. Support Individual Growth: Champion each other's personal growth. Encourage pursuits that align with individual passions and shared dreams.

5. Navigate Conflict with Grace: Conflict is a chance to deepen understanding. Approach disagreements with empathy, seeking mutual solutions.

6. Celebrate Intimacy: Nurture emotional intimacy and express physical affection. These gestures strengthen your romantic bond.

7. Learn from Mistakes: Mistakes and failures are lessons in disguise. Embrace them as opportunities for growth and resilience.

Guidance for Cultivating the Marriage Mindset:
1. Prioritize Connection: Make time for each other. Engage in activities that nurture connection and shared experiences.

2. Be Open to Growth: Approach challenges with a positive mindset. Believe that you can overcome obstacles and evolve together.

3. Practice Gratitude: Regularly express gratitude for each other and the journey you're on. Gratitude fosters a sense of appreciation and contentment.

4. Celebrate Milestones: Acknowledge the journey you've taken and celebrate your achievements, both big and small.

5. Seek Support: Don't hesitate to seek guidance from mentors, counselors, or resources that can enrich your relationship.

6. Remember Your Why: Reflect on why you chose each other and the dreams you're building together. Let this anchor you during challenging times.

A Love Story Unveiled:
In the pages of this journey, we've explored the essence of a growth-oriented marriage—a tale of shared dreams, empathy, resilience, and unwavering commitment. As you continue writing your own love story, remember that the marriage mindset is a continuous journey, a commitment to growth and connection that unfolds with every step you take together.

May your love story be one that inspires others, a testament to the power of growth, and a beacon of hope for couples venturing hand in hand into the boundless expanse of love's ever-evolving landscape. So, with hearts full of purpose and love, let us embrace the journey ahead—a journey marked by shared dreams, mutual growth, and a marriage that flourishes in the beauty of growth-oriented love.

Conclusion: Embracing the Ever-Growing Love

As we draw the final curtain on this exploration of the marriage mindset, let us pause to reflect on the profound journey of growth, connection, and shared dreams that we've embarked upon. The tapestry of a thriving relationship is one woven with threads of intention, communication, empathy, and the unwavering commitment to evolve together. This is not a destination reached, but an ongoing journey—a symphony of growth that harmonizes the rhythms of two hearts beating as one.

A Journey Beyond Borders:
The essence of the marriage mindset is not confined to the pages of this guide; it extends into every corner of your relationship. It's the belief that

love is not static but an ever-unfolding story of mutual discovery and growth. It's the realization that through change, challenges, and shared experiences, love deepens and takes root in the fertile soil of unity and understanding.

Prioritizing Growth and Connection:

In the voyage of love, prioritize the cultivation of a growth-oriented mindset. Prioritize open communication that spans beyond words, empathy that transcends differences, and the recognition that each challenge is an invitation to emerge stronger and wiser. Nurturing your bond requires effort, intention, and a genuine commitment to fostering mutual growth.

Embrace Change with Open Arms:

Change is not an adversary; it's a dance partner that invites you to move in harmony with life's rhythms. Embrace it with open arms, knowing that every twist and turn is an opportunity to learn, adapt, and cultivate deeper love.

A Love That Evolves:

The marriage mindset is an ever-evolving journey, an adventure that transcends time and place. It's an ode to shared dreams, a symphony of empathy, and a celebration of the courage to face challenges hand in hand. As you continue your journey, remember that the tapestry you're weaving is unique—a masterpiece that only the two of you can create.

Continue Writing Your Love Story:

With each sunrise, you're given a new page to craft your love story. Prioritize growth, communication, and a positive approach to challenges. Be the authors of a tale that inspires, a love that withstands the test of time, and a partnership that is evergreen, ever-evolving.

So, as you step into the chapters of your shared future, let the marriage mindset be your compass, guiding you through the chapters of growth, connection, and love that are yet to be written. May your journey be one of infinite discovery, unyielding unity, and the radiant beauty that blooms from

THE EVER-UNFOLDING TALE: EMBRACING THE JOURNEY OF GROWTH...

a love that knows no bounds.

www.ingramcontent.com/pod-product-compliance
Lightning Source LLC
LaVergne TN
LVHW010441070526
838199LV00066B/6120